LITTLE TREES, BIG SKY

Portrait
of a
Northern
Wilderness

A

PHOTOGRAPHIC

INTERPRETATION

BY

TIM HAUF

Text by Conger Beasley Jr.

Little Trees, Big Sky
Portrait of a Northern Wilderness
A Photographic Interpretation by Tim Hauf

Published by Tim Hauf Photography

Photography by Tim Hauf

Text by Conger Beasley Jr.

Book design by Peggy Ferris Design, Santa Barbara, CA

ISBN 0-9659688-3-9
First Printing May, 2000
Printed and bound in Korea

Previous Spread: Arctic cotton-grass *(Eriophorum sp.),*
along the Thlewiaza River.
Above: Evening light on the Hayes River as it enters
the Hudson Bay lowlands.
Opposite above: Fireweed *(Epilobium angustifolium),*
one of the first plants to follow a fire.

Acknowledgements

Publishing a book of this type requires the involvement of many dedicated and enthusiastic people and organisations in order to obtain the photos, properly identify the subjects, and verify the accuracy of the information presented. Sincere thanks to the following for their assistance and support:

Colette Fontaine and Jan Collins of Travel Manitoba, for their assistance in trip planning, and for their confidence in my photographic abilities.

Virginia Petch, Ph.D. of Northern Lights Heritage Services, for writing the foreword and for providing a unique insight into the cultural and archaeological aspects of the wilderness.

Elizabeth Punter, consultant botanist, for invaluable assistance in plant identification.

Heather Groom, physical geologist with the Manitoba Department of Mines and Energy, for providing information regarding geological features.

Conger Beasley Jr., for his ability to capture the essence of the Northern Wilderness through his unique writing style.

Monica Campbell-Hoppe of the Canadian Consulate General Office, for her assistance in making arrangements with AIR CANADA for transportation to Manitoba.

Peggy Ferris, for her design skills that are necessary in the publication of a book of this nature.

Special thanks also to the following tour operators and outfitters, for their co-operation in making these trips possible:

Steve Miller of Midwest Helicopters, Ltd.; Len Smith of Tundra Buggy Tours; Mike Macri of Sea North Tours; David Koritko of Wilderness Odysseys, Ltd.; Brad Stoneman of Northwest Wilderness Adventures; Garth Duncan of Raven Eye Outfitters; Dan Benoit of Boreal Wilderness Guides; Mike Reimer of Seal River Lodge.

Moody depths of the boreal forest.

Contents

Foreword

Northern Canada, a land of rugged and uncompromising beauty, is dominated by the great Canadian Shield. This magnificent landscape was sculptured by the last ice age, which left deep furrows etched into the rock's surface. These channels have become the pathways of the many river systems, all of which drain into Hudson Bay. From the air, the land resembles a multitude of water puddles after a rainstorm. From the ground, the dense coniferous forests, wetlands and rugged relief quickly dispel any thoughts of a walk through the park. The North is not for the faint of heart! But to trek across the eskers, feel the spray of the rapids, see the eagle soar and breathe the scent of a spruce forest is to know that you have truly experienced life as it was in the not-so-distant past.

The climatic variability contributes to the kinds of vegetation, and hence animal resources that one can expect to see. Often, one is so concerned with one's own survival, that many of the less conspicuous and humbler life forms are overlooked. These hardy denizens of the North have developed a foolproof means of dealing with the vagaries of nature in order that their survival, and those of their predators, is guaranteed.

As an archaeologist, I have had the privilege to explore much of the North that is illustrated in this descriptive collection of photographs and text. One would think that after a dozen or so treks into "the bush" the thrill of the North would wear off. On the contrary, each trip is a renewal of spirit, a chance to get myself back on track and realign my values. It is my personal "natural health spa".

Tim Hauf has captured the essence of the North on the following pages. He illustrates the delicate beauty and the harsh reality of life in the North. He illuminates and reminds us of all things great and small—all the many facets of the diamond of the northern landscape.

I am privileged to know Tim and the gentle and thoughtful manner in which this delightful book was created. Enjoy!

Virginia Petch, Ph.D.
Archaeologist
Northern Lights Heritage Services

Opposite: Evening colour on Oxford Lake, Hayes River.
Above: Prairie crocus or pasque flower *(Anemone patens)*, Manitoba's official flower.

Wilderness Pure and Simple

What do we take away with us from any given place? Sights, sounds, thoughts, impressions. Something less tangible as well… a feeling, a taste, a residue; the diminuendo of a ravishing chord that once reverberated between our ears, and that echoes still, but faintly, in a muted tone.

I've been to Manitoba five times, and I hope to return a few times more. It's not a place that most folks single out as their primary destination. British Columbia gets the nod for that, the Yukon, Jasper and Banff National Parks, maybe the Maritime Provinces. The big-ticket locales that bowl you over with their spectacular scenery.

Manitoba exhudes a different appeal. It's reticent, low-key, undemonstrative. It boasts a population of less than two million and enough square kilometres in which to hide all of New England and most of Pennsylvania, New York, Michigan, and Ohio. The majority of the landmass lies concealed under boreal forest, domed by outcroppings of granitic rock. Apart from the prairies southwest of Winnipeg, not much of the land is arable. North of the 54th parallel, it's mostly trees, rivers, lakes, and muskeg. The forest floor is carpeted with reindeer lichen which crackles underfoot like a string of firecrackers. The native people up there–Cree, Dene, Anishinabe–hunt caribou, chop wood, and trap fur-bearing animals as they've done for centuries. They also ride snowmobiles, fly aeroplanes, watch television, and work with computers. But the land still dominates. The great boreal silence persists with a profundity that no machine can shatter.

I got my first glimpse of this landscape one afternoon as the single-engine DeHavilland Beaver lifted off the water at Matheson Island on Lake Winnipeg, carrying Tim Hauf and myself out to the Pigeon River. The extent of it left me dumbfounded. Threaded with interlocking lakes and rivers, the land unfolded to the horizon in a gritty, dark-green mat of pines, spruce, and hardwoods, interspersed with bogs and marshes. There were no villages, towns, or settlements that I could see. There were few signs of human life anywhere.

Opposite: Portage trail along the Pigeon River, Atikaki Provincial Wilderness Park.
Above: Caribou trail along the Robertson Esker.

As a Midwesterner from the States, such a vista, located in the centre of Canada, was a revelation. Down home, my eye was accustomed to myriad forms marking the land–squares, circles, rectangles–the tight, interlocking geometry of cultivated property. Gertrude Stein, flying over Ohio and Indiana in the 1930s, looked down upon this orderly layout with its rigid cubist configurations and whispered, "Picasso was right! Picasso was right!"

The Manitoba I viewed that memorable afternoon in 1995 was blissfully free of any such superimposed grid. It was wilderness pure and simple-- coarse, rough, messy, uncompromising. Dark country, wild, splashed with green sinkholes, inhabited by furry animals, forested with stands of spruce,

Above: Yellow evening primrose *(Oenothera biennis),* Pigeon
River, Atikaki Provincial Wilderness Park.
Below: Pigeon River, Atikaki Provincial Wilderness Park.

Morning light, Pigeon River,
Atikaki Provincial Wilderness Park.

Above:
Wild rice *(Zizania aquatica)*, Atikaki Provincial
Wilderness Park.
Opposite:
Yellow pond-lily *(Nuphar variegata)*, Atikaki Provincial
Wilderness Park.

Water slathering through the steep gorge of
Asineewakkayhigun Rapids, Bloodvein River,
Atikaki Provincial Wilderness Park.

Top: Pine Point Rapids,
Whiteshell Provincial Park.
Bottom: Bloodvein River,
Atikaki Provincial Wilderness Park.

Above: Reindeer lichen *(Cladina rangiferina)* and hair-cap moss *(Polytrichum juniperinum)*, Atikaki Provincial Wilderness Park.
Opposite: British soldiers *(Cladonia sp.)*.

Black bear *(Ursus americanus),*
Atikaki Provincial Wilderness Park.

The Seal River's outstanding natural beauty is the
primary reason it has been included in the Canadian
Heritage River System.

Burnt-out forest, with smoke from a new fire visible
on the horizon.

Arctic cotton-grass and fireweed.

The morning air is crisp and still at minus 40 degrees.

Above left: Prickly rose *(Rosa acicularis).*
Above middle: Tall lungwort *(Mertensia paniculata).*
Above right: Stemless raspberry *(Rubus acaulis).*

Previous pages: Rainbow following an intense
summer thunderstorm.
Opposite: Caribou antler, Great Island, Seal River.
Above left: Cobwebs, Robertson Esker.
Above middle: Bear-claw marks along the Seal River.
Above right: Wolf den, Seal River.

Paktikonika Rapids, on the Hayes River,
Manitoba's largest untamed river.

Still water just before Neesootakuskaywin Rapids,
Hayes River.

Bog where the Robertson Esker crosses the
Winnberg River.

Above left: Three-leaved Solomon's-seal
(Smilacina trifolia).
Above middle: Mountain club-moss
(Lycopodium selago).
Above right: Wood horsetail
(Equisetum sylvaticum).

The swift-flowing Hayes River is lined with steep clay
slopes as it approaches the Hudson Bay lowlands.

The serenity of a quiet summer evening is reflected in
puddles along the Seal River.

Round-leaved sundew *(Drosera rotundifolia)*.

Top: Marsh cinquefoil *(Potentilla palustris).*
Bottom: Mushroom pronging from a bed of lichen.

Twilight, Seal River.

Opposite and Above: Winter sunrise.

Migrating barren-ground caribou
(Rangifer tarandus groenlandicus).

Cloudberries *(Rubus chamaemorus)* and Arctic cotton-grass add a splash of colour to the tundra.

Sunlight filtering through Arctic cotton-grass.

Least willow *(Salix herbacea).*

No roads, no trees, no people. Just a wide river
meandering across an endless horizon.

This large rock along the Seal River is visible for miles
on the flat terrain. Aboriginal people and early
explorers once used it as a navigational marker.

Tundra nudging up against the transition zone, with
forest in the distance.

Above left: Bog rosemary *(Andromeda polifolia)*.
Above middle: Alpine bearberry
(Arctostaphylos alpina).
Above right: Bog bilberry *(Vaccinium uliginosum)*.

Marsh ragwort *(Senecio congestus)* adds colour to the otherwise drab mud flats of Hudson Bay.

Above: Rocks, smoothed by glacial action, provide
cover for polar bears during warm summer days.
Opposite: Geese and other birds nest and feed on the
nutrient-rich Hudson Bay lowlands.

Previous pages; left: Close-up, sea-shore camomile
(Matricaria ambigua).
Previous pages; right: A colourful palette of
summer flowers.
Above: The ghostly beluga or white whale
(Delphinapterus leucas Pallas) is often called the
"canary of the sea" because of its vocalisations.

Paddling across a tranquil lake in Atikaki Provincial
Wilderness Park.

Camping along the Seal River.

Above: Campsite.
Following spread: Winter road, Reindeer Lake.